DESTINATION:
VENUS

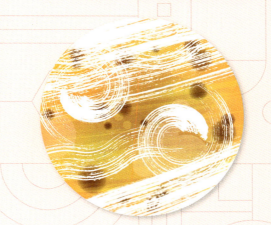

SALLY SPRAY AND
MARK RUFFLE

First published in Great Britain in 2023
by Wayland
© Hodder and Stoughton Limited, 2023

HB ISBN: 978 1 5263 2094 0
PB ISBN: 978 1 5263 2095 7

Editor: Paul Rockett
Design and illustration: Mark Ruffle
www.rufflebrothers.com

MIX
Paper from
responsible sources
FSC® C104740
www.fsc.org
FSC

Printed in Dubai

Wayland
An imprint of Hachette Children's Group
Part of Hodder & Stoughton
Carmelite House
50 Victoria Embankment
London EC4Y 0DZ

An Hachette UK company
www.hachette.co.uk
www.hachettechildrens.co.uk

The website addresses (URLs) included in this book were valid at the time of going to press. However, it is possible that contents or addresses may have changed since the publication of this book. No responsibility for any such changes can be accepted by either the author or the Publisher.

Picture credits:
Page 30 JPL/NASA;
page 31 JPL/NASA; Goddard/NASA

SAFETY PRECAUTIONS

We recommend adult supervision at all times while doing the experiments in this book. Always be aware that ingredients may contain allergens, so check the packaging for allergens if there is a risk of an allergic reaction. Anyone with a known allergy must avoid these.

- Wear an apron and cover surfaces.
- Tie back long hair.
- Ask an adult for help with cutting.
- Check all ingredients for allergens.
- Clear up all spills straight away.

Contents

Meet the team

Dr Bott

Mo

Stella

Max

Xing

Melody

Welcome to Space Station Academy, the amazing interstellar school that travels through space. Come on board and learn about our solar system.

Today, the Space Academy is nearing Venus with its swirling gas clouds. The students are busy baking and have some clouds of their own to deal with.

Look how beautiful Venus looks – it's so pretty covered in swirly patterns.

Can't wait to go and see it close-up.

What a mess! What's happened to the atmosphere in here and where is that smoke coming from?

It's not looking good.

You can clean this up while I tell you about Venus.

Venus is the second planet from the Sun. It is Earth's next door neighbour, about 61 million km away.

But, Earth actually spends more time closer to Mercury. As Mercury has such a fast orbit it passes by Earth three times for each Venus orbit.

It's a rocky planet, like Mercury and Earth, but has layers of thick cloud in its atmosphere.

Our cake's pretty rocky.

Later, in the space pod.

 Hold on tight! Venus is up ahead.

 It's not as big as I had imagined.

 The diameter of Venus is 12,104 km, just a tiny bit bigger than Earth. If Earth was wearing a coat made from the outside of Venus, it wouldn't be able to do all the buttons up.

It's very beautiful, look at the colours. And it's so bright!

From Earth you can see it without a telescope. The atmosphere on Venus is so thick, it reflects 70 per cent of the light that reaches it from the Sun, making it one of the brightest objects in Earth's night sky.

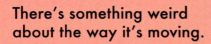

There's something weird about the way it's moving.

It's going the wrong way!

Venus spins in the opposite direction to all the other planets in our solar system. Scientists aren't sure why this happens.

So, on Venus the Sun rises in the west and goes down in the east, the opposite way to Earth – awesome!

It's like being in a mixer!

The winds are very strong at the poles, but calmer around the middle of the planet, at the equator.

This is fun!

11

The clouds are so thick and yellow we can't see where we going.

That's because the atmosphere on Venus is very different to Earth's. Carbon dioxide (CO_2) makes up 95 per cent of the atmosphere here. On Earth the atmosphere contains around 1 per cent CO_2.

CO_2 particles capture energy and heat from the Sun, which is trapped in the atmosphere. This makes the planet's temperature rise. It's called the greenhouse effect and causes global warming.

Greenhouse Effect

Sun

Seconds later, on Venus.

Ooops! I think we made a bit of a hasty landing.

There's smoke, Dr B!

For the second time today!

Don't worry, kids, that's nothing to worry about. Now into the space bubbles and out onto Venus.

Space bubbles?!

The pressure on the planet's surface is as strong as being 1 km underwater on Earth. It's so strong you'd be crushed flat. And it's so hot you'd be burnt to a crisp.

A Stella pancake!

A flat Max!

Venus is a very interesting planet. It spins verrrrry slowwwwwly and this slow spin affects its shape, making it one of the roundest planets in our solar system.

If it spins so slowly does it have really long days?

Yes, a day here – that's one spin on its axis – lasts 243 Earth days. So, it could have daylight for 121.5 Earth days and one night could last 121.5 days.

Even I couldn't sleep that long!

But, a Venus year – that's one orbit around the Sun – takes 225 days.

Let's stop for a while and look closely at the landscape. What can you see?

I can't see any craters.

It looks very hot and dry and not as pretty down here as it is from space. This ground is smooth, but there are mountains over there.

The surface is smooth because it has been covered with lava, like icing on a cake. Strangely, the surface is not as old as other planets. Some parts of Venus could be as young as 150 million years old whereas most planet surfaces are billions of years old.

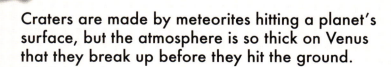

Craters are made by meteorites hitting a planet's surface, but the atmosphere is so thick on Venus that they break up before they hit the ground.

Scientists have discovered a gas called phosphine in the clouds. On Earth, this gas is produced by living organisms, so out there in the thick, thick clouds, there could be some sort of tiny microbe life forms.

Oh, cool! I wonder what the microbes look like?

Would they eat our cake?

Shield volcano

They don't have explosive eruptions – lava oozes from the centre and moves slowly outwards over the edges.

Pancake dome

These volcanoes are large and flat, that's how they get their name! We don't get these on Earth.

Come on, let's go and have a look in one.

Is that a good idea?

The biggest volcano is called Maat Mons – it's 8 km high. That's 800 m shorter than Mount Everest on Earth.

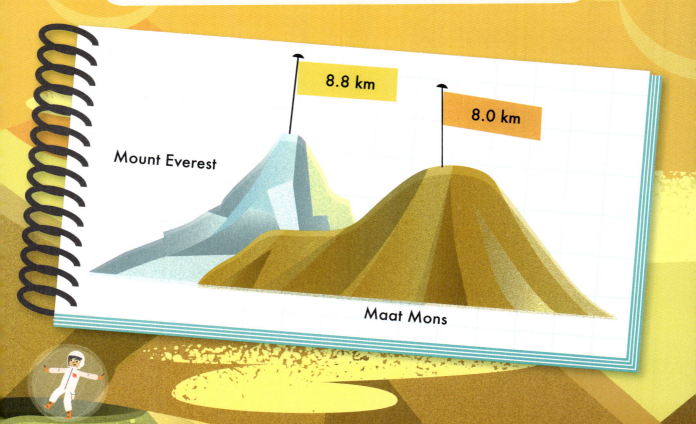

8.8 km

8.0 km

Mount Everest

Maat Mons

Hurry up! The view is amazing up here!

24

I'm feeling quite hungry after that adventure. Where's our cake?

Welcome back space cadets – good to have you home.

Is that it? Mo, it looks amazing!

Space Academy Activities

The Space Academy gang have been so inspired by their mission to Venus, they wanted to find out more. Will you join them?

Dr Bott's Space Experiment

Venus is covered with volcanoes, have a go at making your own. You might want to try this outside. Ask an adult for permission to do this activity.

Equipment
- Paper, card, modelling clay, paint to decorate
- Food colouring
- Water
- Bicarbonate of soda
- White vinegar
- Bottle
- Jar and cup

Method
You can make a volcano in a jar. Make it super-realistic by hiding the jar in a paper cone, a modelling clay volcano or a papier-mâché mountain.

Mix 1 tablespoon of bicarbonate of soda with 1 tbsp of washing up liquid and 2 tbsp water. Pour into the jar.

In a separate cup mix half a cup of white vinegar with a few drops of food colouring. Pour the vinegar into the jar.

Outcomes
What happens when the vinegar is added?

Experiment variations
Try the experiment again altering the amounts of bicarbonate of soda, vinegar and water. Record your results.

Melody's Venus Fact

When Venus is seen from the Earth it has phases like the Earth's Moon, when we see different amounts of its surface.

When Venus is in front of the Sun some of it is in shadow, so we just see a crescent of Venus. As it passes behind the Sun, we see more of the planet.

The scientist, Galileo, observed this in 1610. It proved the theory that all the planets in the solar system orbit the Sun.

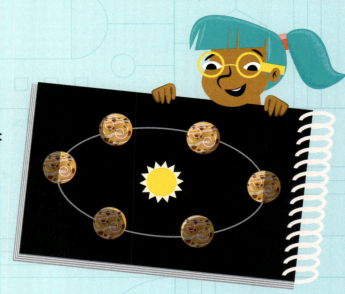

Max's Extra Venus Fact

The biggest volcano on Venus is Maat Mons. The biggest on Earth is called Mauna Loa – it's 4,169 m high and is in Hawaii.

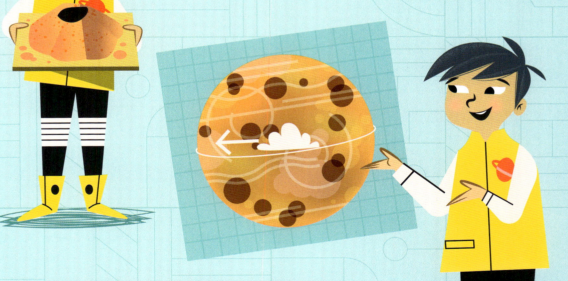

Xing's Venus Maths Problem

If the circumference of Venus is 38,025 km, how many hours would it take a cloud to go all the way round the planet being pushed by a 338 km/h wind? How many Earth days is this? Round up your answer.

Stella's Venus Picture Gallery

Come and see the images in my marvellous Venus picture gallery.

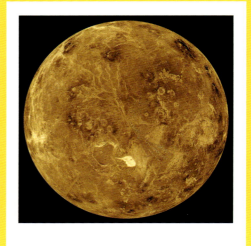

Approaching Venus, this is the view of the swirling clouds in the atmosphere.

Under the clouds, the rocky, volcanic surface looks like this.

Mo's Research Project

Find out when the next research mission to Venus is and what scientists plan to investigate. What would you like them to research?

Mission to Venus

A closer view of the ground and a volcano called Sapas Mons.

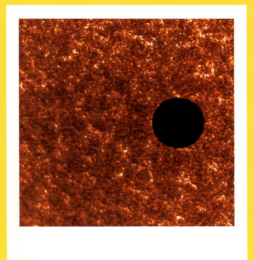

Here is Venus orbiting the fiery Sun and absorbing lots of heat.

Further information

Wonderful websites

nasa.gov/kidsclub/index.html
esa.int/kids/en/home
spaceplace.nasa.gov/all-about-venus/en/
kids.nationalgeographic.com/space/article/mission-to-venus

Brilliant books

Dr Maggie's Grand Tour of the Solar System by Dr Maggie Aderin-Pocock (Buster Books, 2019)
So Many Questions About Space by Sally Spray (Wayland, 2022)
Wonders of the Night Sky by Professor Raman Prinja (Wayland, 2022)

Glossary

atmosphere – the layer of gas surrounding a planet
axis – the imaginary line around which an object, such as a planet, rotates
circumference – the measurement all the way around a circle or sphere
crater – a large, bowl-shaped hole in the surface of something, such as a moon, or the top of a volcano
diameter – the measurement across the middle of a sphere or circle
global warming – the process of warming a planet, when heated gases cannot escape the atmosphere
interstellar – describes something that is located or happens between stars
meteor – a space rock that appears as a streak of light as it falls through the atmosphere
meteorite – a space rock that has fallen through a planet's atmosphere and landed on its surface
microbes – living things that are too small to be seen without a microscope
moon – a natural body that orbits a planet
orbit – the path a planet or moon takes around a star or planet
pressure – the amount of push force on something
scientist – a person who researches, tests and learns about the natural world
solar system – the Sun and the objects in orbit around it

Index